PYRAMID

Author:

Henrietta McCall
studied Egyptology at Oxford
University in England. She is
the author of *Mesopotamian
Myths* and has edited numerous
children's books on ancient
Egypt. She is also a member
of the Council of the British
Museum Society.

Artist:

David Antram was
born in Brighton, England, in
1958. He studied at Eastbourne
College of Art and then worked
in advertising for 15 years before
becoming a full-time artist. He
has illustrated many children's
non-fiction books.

Editors:

Stephen Haynes
Caroline Coleman

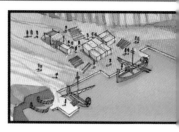

Published in Great Britain in MMXIV by
Book House, an imprint of
The Salariya Book Company Ltd
25 Marlborough Place, Brighton, BN1 1UB
www.salariya.com
www.book-house.co.uk

ISBN 978-1-909645-69-1

SALARIYA

A CIP Catalogue record for this book is available
from the British Library.

Printed and bound in China.
Printed on paper from sustainable sources.

PAPER FROM
SUSTAINABLE
FORESTS

Visit our website at **www.book-house.co.uk** or
www.salariya.com for free electronic versions of:
You Wouldn't Want to be an Egyptian Mummy!
You Wouldn't Want to be a Roman Gladiator!
Avoid Joining Shackleton's Polar Expedition!
Avoid Sailing on a 19th-Century Whaling Ship!

PYRAMID

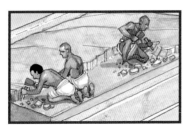

Written by
HENRIETTA McCALL

Illustrated by
DAVID ANTRAM

Created and designed by
DAVID SALARIYA

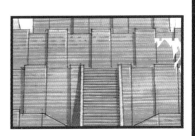

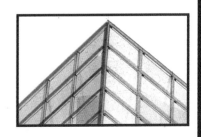

BOOK HOUSE
a SALARIYA imprint

Contents

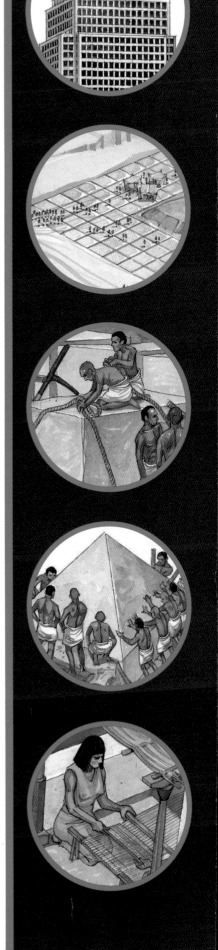

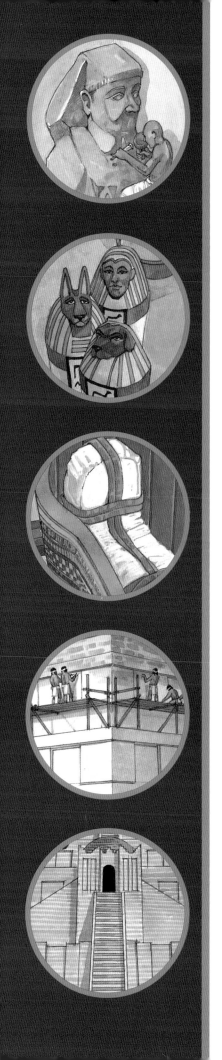

Assyrian ziggurat

Ziggurat at Ur

The first Sumerian ziggurats were built at the cities of Ur, Eridu, Uruk, and Nippur. Babylon's most famous ziggurat, named Etemenanki, was so tall that it was thought to be the Tower of Babel described in the Bible.

Pyramids in Nubia

Pyramid in ancient Rome

Etemenanki ziggurat

Pyramids around the world

The first pyramids were built in ancient Egypt but pyramids were also found in Nubia, ancient Rome, Central America and the Far East. Similar structures, called **ziggurats**, were built in ancient **Mesopotamia** (modern Iraq). These early pyramids were burial sites or places of worship.

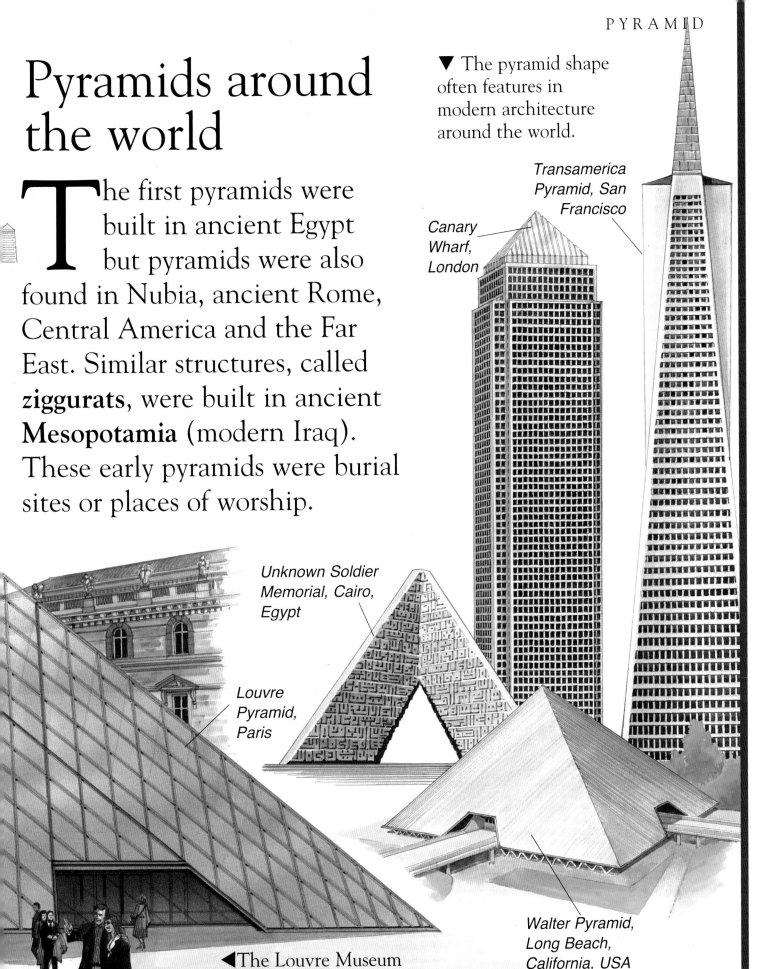

▼ The pyramid shape often features in modern architecture around the world.

Transamerica Pyramid, San Francisco

Canary Wharf, London

Unknown Soldier Memorial, Cairo, Egypt

Louvre Pyramid, Paris

Walter Pyramid, Long Beach, California, USA

◄ The Louvre Museum Pyramid is made of steel and glass. It is 20 m high.

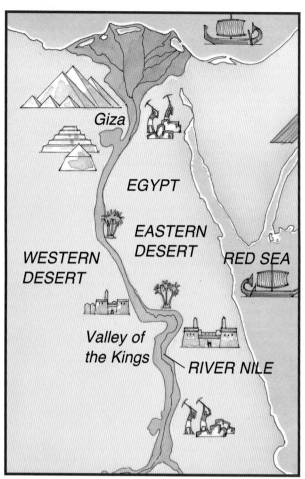

Ancient Egypt

Hathor   Horus

Egypt's pyramids were burial sites for **pharaohs** (kings). A pharaoh's tomb was sealed deep within the pyramid, along with his treasures and all his needs for the afterlife. Over time, tomb robbers have stolen most of the treasure hidden in pyramids.

◀ The earliest Egyptian burials were simple pits in the sand.

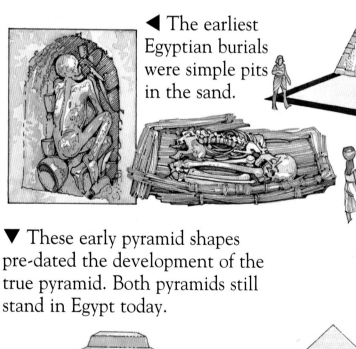

Mastaba

▲ The first attempt to build a pyramid consisted of a flat platform called a **mastaba** with a tomb underground.

▼ These early pyramid shapes pre-dated the development of the true pyramid. Both pyramids still stand in Egypt today.

The Step Pyramid
Saqqara

The Bent Pyramid
Dashur

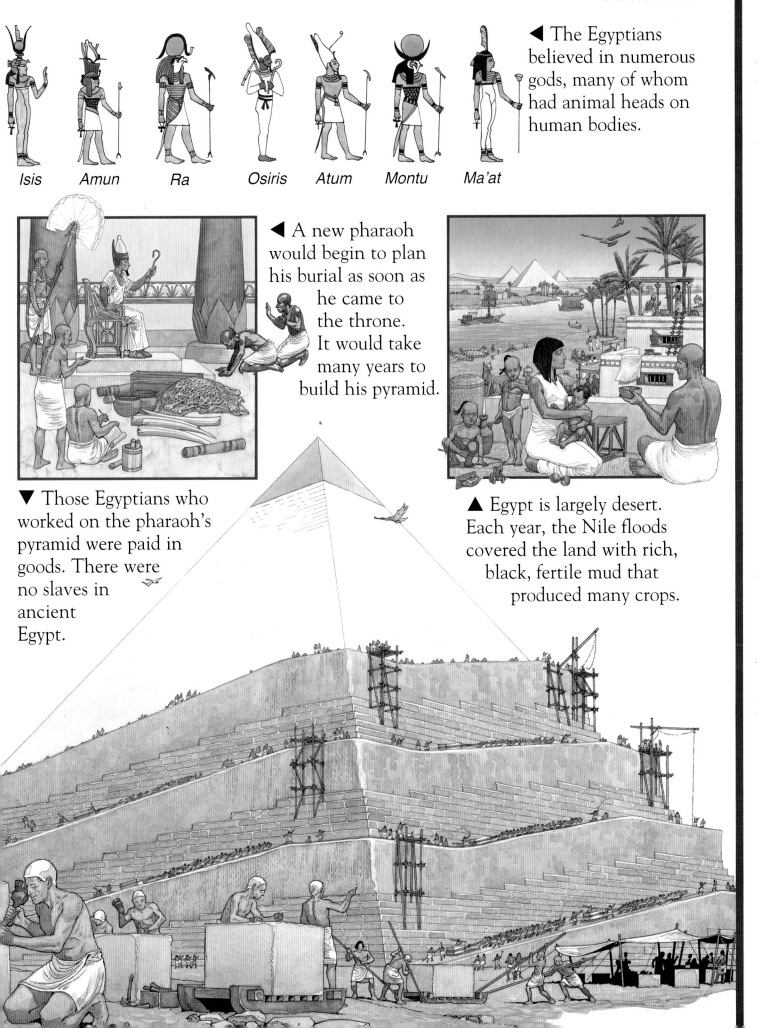

Isis *Amun* *Ra* *Osiris* *Atum* *Montu* *Ma'at*

◀ The Egyptians believed in numerous gods, many of whom had animal heads on human bodies.

◀ A new pharaoh would begin to plan his burial as soon as he came to the throne. It would take many years to build his pyramid.

▼ Those Egyptians who worked on the pharaoh's pyramid were paid in goods. There were no slaves in ancient Egypt.

▲ Egypt is largely desert. Each year, the Nile floods covered the land with rich, black, fertile mud that produced many crops.

Laying foundations

A pharaoh's pyramid site had to be large enough to accommodate a Mortuary Temple; smaller pyramids for his family; **a boat pit**; a causeway to the Nile; and areas to house the workmen and store the quarried stone.

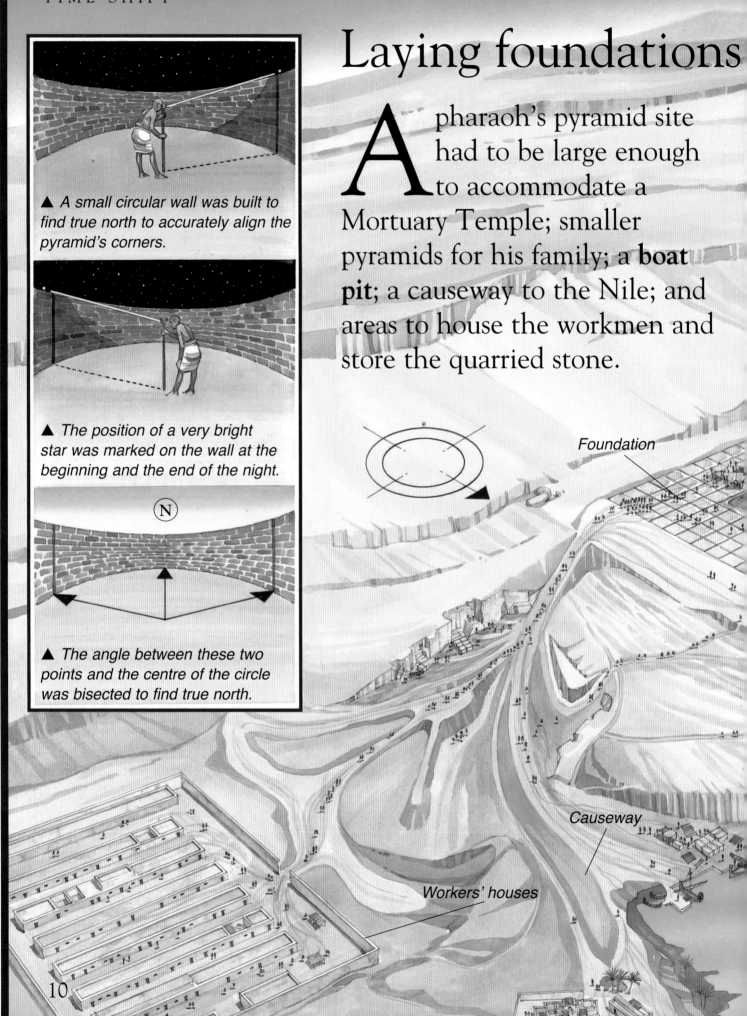

▲ A small circular wall was built to find true north to accurately align the pyramid's corners.

▲ The position of a very bright star was marked on the wall at the beginning and the end of the night.

▲ The angle between these two points and the centre of the circle was bisected to find true north.

Foundation

Causeway

Workers' houses

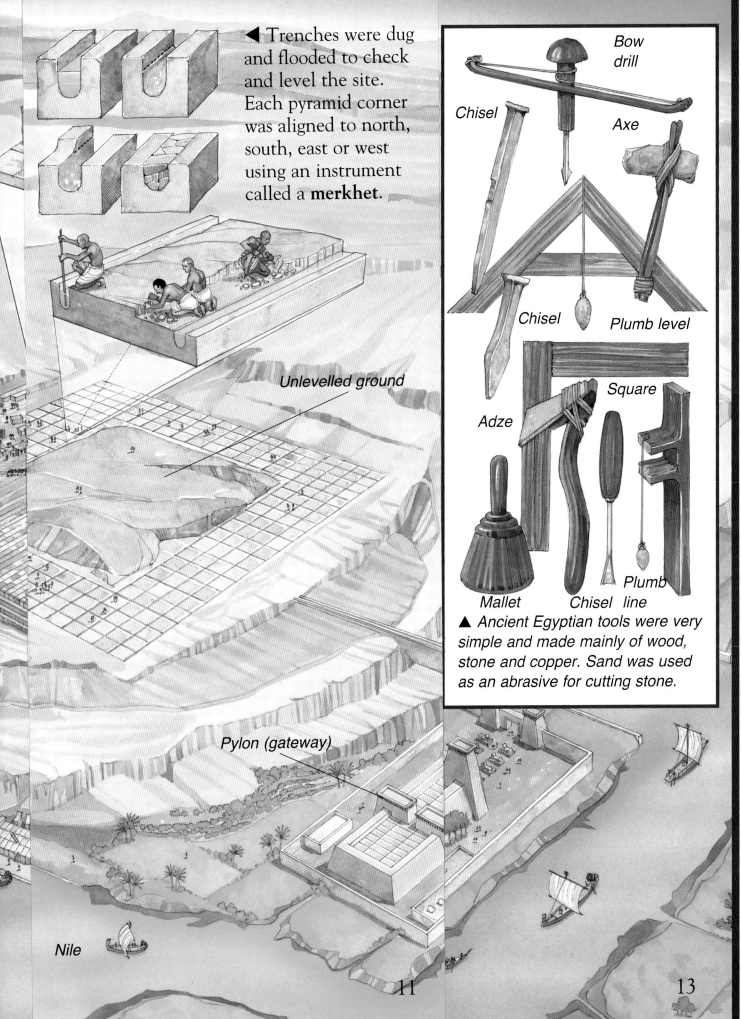

◄ Trenches were dug and flooded to check and level the site. Each pyramid corner was aligned to north, south, east or west using an instrument called a **merkhet**.

Bow drill

Chisel

Axe

Chisel

Plumb level

Adze

Square

Mallet   Chisel   Plumb line

▲ Ancient Egyptian tools were very simple and made mainly of wood, stone and copper. Sand was used as an abrasive for cutting stone.

Unlevelled ground

Pylon (gateway)

Nile

11

13

Quarrying the stone

T he Nile floods allowed the huge blocks of stone to be ferried straight from the quarry across to the pyramid site.

▼ Men dragged the blocks by rope or on wooden rollers from the quarry to the barge.

Quarry

Stone

▼ The blocks were marked out with chiselled lines. Wooden wedges were hammered in and soaked with water. As the wood expanded, it split the stone.

Wooden rollers

▼ The top of the pyramid would be completed with a gilded capstone, called a **pyramidion**.

◄ A pyramid structure is formed with stepped platforms. The steps are then packed out to form a true pyramid. It is then cased in fine, white limestone.

A pyramid rises

The quarried stone blocks were dragged from the boat to the pyramid. Teams of men then hauled them up the ramps and into position.

▼ Pottery drinking vessels were baked in the workshop kiln.

◀ Statues were hewn from fine-quality stone such as **alabaster**.

▲ Wood was not plentiful in Egypt and was brought from Lebanon.

The royal workshops

A vast workforce built the Great Pyramid. Workers' villages, unearthed by archaeologists, have revealed much about everyday life on a pyramid site.

◄ All houses in Egypt were made of sun-dried mud bricks.

◄ Women wove coarse linen into simple garments.

▼ The women baked flat bread on hot stones.

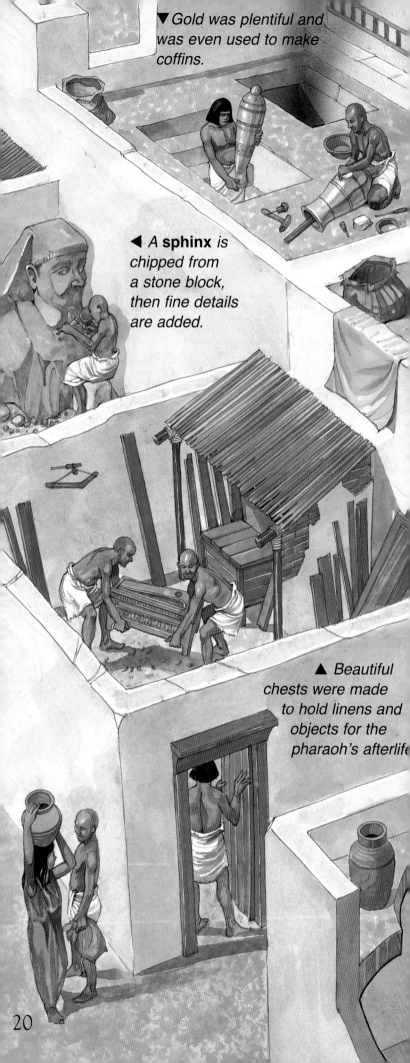

▼ Gold was plentiful and was even used to make coffins.

◄ A **sphinx** is chipped from a stone block, then fine details are added.

▲ Beautiful chests were made to hold linens and objects for the pharaoh's afterlife

20

Skilled workers

Egypt's craftsmen were highly skilled jewellers and gold workers. Artists' colours were ground from stones and minerals such as bright blue lapis lazuli.

▲ An ancient Egyptian's diet was very healthy – plenty of fibre and very little fat.

▶ Baskets were used to store or transport most things – even babies.

▼ Archaeologists have found many sandals on the pyramid site.

21

Making a mummy

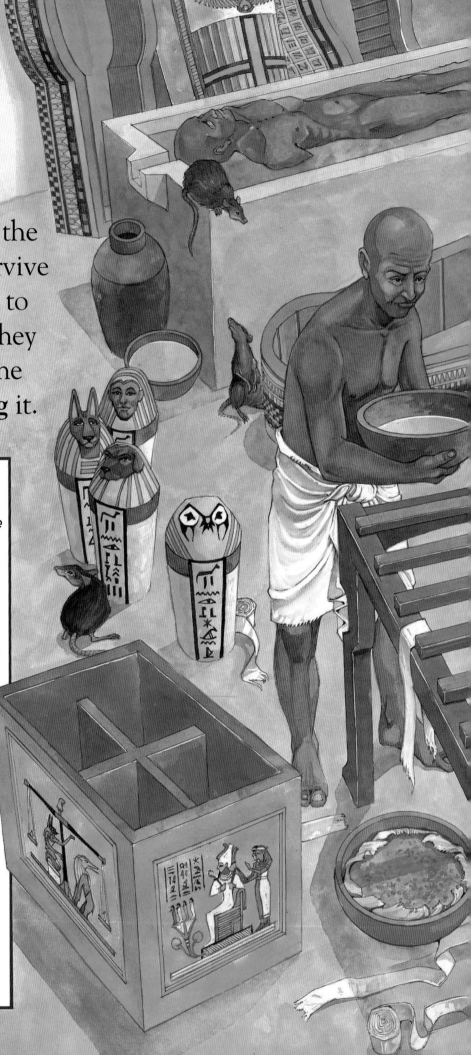

The Egyptians believed that the body must survive death intact in order to enjoy the afterlife. They learned to preserve the body by **mummifying** it.

(a) In the House of Purification, the body was laid on a slab.

(b) The brains were hooked out through the nostrils.

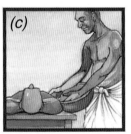

(c) The internal organs were extracted and the cavity was washed and stitched up.

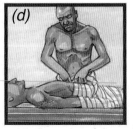

(d) After 70 days in dry **natron** salts, the body was wrapped in bandages.

22

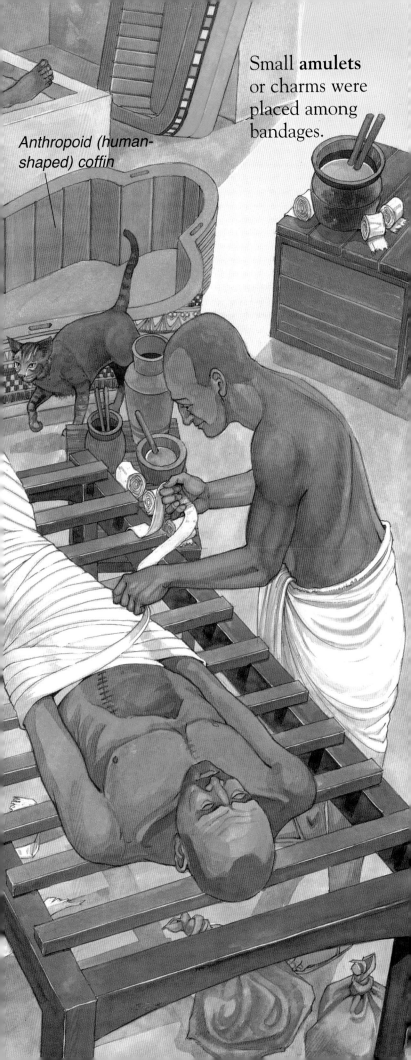

Small **amulets** or charms were placed among bandages.

Anthropoid (human-shaped) coffin

Canopic jar

Canopic chest

24

Coffin lid

Anubis *mask*

▲ *The mummified pharaoh was ferried across the river to his Mortuary Temple.*

A royal funeral

The body was laid in a beautifully decorated wooden coffin. This was placed inside a stone **sarcophagus**. The internal organs were sealed in **canopic jars**.

▼ At the Mortuary Temple, the dead pharaoh was prepared for his final journey to the afterlife.

Central American pyramids

About 2,500 years later, pyramids were built by the Incas in Peru, the Aztecs in Mexico, and the Maya in modern-day Honduras and Guatemala. The Mayan pyramid at Chichén Itzá was built about AD 1100.

▶ The main pyramid at Chichén Itzá is called the Castillo.

▲ Three well-known pyramids of Central America: Tenochtitlán, Chichén Itzá and Etowah.

► The Great Temple at Tenochtitlán was a stepped pyramid on a platform. Its two shrines were dedicated to Aztec gods.

The Aztecs believed in human sacrifice. Terrible ceremonies took place before the shrines of the Great Temple where priests would rip open the victim's chest to give its heart to the gods.

▼ The city of Etowah was at its greatest about AD 1200. Its power was reflected by its grand palaces and temples.

◄ The Castillo has 365 steps – the number of days in a year.

▼ The temple of Dhammayangyi is at Bagan, once a great walled city and the capital of old Burma.

Stupa

▼ The stepped pyramid of Dhammayangyi is topped by a bell-dome, or *stupa*. It was built by King Narathu. The temple has identical pillars at each corner and has shrines on either side of the arched front entrance.

Dhammayangyi Temple

Asian pyramids

Many of Asia's temples and places of worship are dedicated to Buddhism. The Buddha was born in Nepal in the 6th century BC. The Buddhist's code, called **dharma**, is based on principles of non-violence and mutual respect.

▼ Borobudur in central Java was built around AD 800. Over a million blocks of dark grey volcanic stone were used to construct it. On the upper three circular terraces are 72 small stupas, each one covered in stone latticework. On the very top terrace is a 30 m high stupa.

▶ Inside each of the 72 stupas is a statue of the Buddha sitting cross-legged with his hands upturned in his lap.

Borobudur

Useful words

Alabaster
Fine, translucent limestone.

Amulets
Small charms, usually hidden in the mummy bandages, to protect the dead in the afterlife.

Anubis
The ancient Egyptian jackal-headed god of the dead, associated with embalming and mummification.

Boat pit
A pit in which a boat was buried for use in the afterlife.

Canopic jars
Special jars to store the internal organs of a mummified person.

Dharma
The Buddhist code of good conduct.

Mastaba
Arabic word meaning 'bench', used to describe a type of ancient Egyptian tomb.

Merkhet
An ancient instrument used to make astronomical measurements.

Mesopotamia
The area between the rivers Tigris and Euphrates (Modern Iraq).

Mummifying
The ancient Egyptian way of preserving a dead body so that it would survive in the afterlife.

Natron
A chemical compound of salts used in the mummification process.

Pharaoh
A title given to Ancient Egyptian kings.

Plumb line
A length of string with a weight at one end, used by builders to achieve a true vertical line.

Pyramidion
The capstone, often gilded to reflect the sun's rays, that is set on the summit of a pyramid.

Sarcophagus
An outermost stone coffin containing one or more wooden coffins. Some sarcophagi are of colossal size and carved both inside and out.

Sphinx
A mythical creature with the head of a human on the body of a lion.

Ziggurat
A Mesopotamian form of stepped pyramid with a temple on the top.

Pyramid facts

Our word *pyramid* is derived from a Greek word 'pyramis', which was a form of wheat cake, presumably shaped like a pyramid.

Pharaoh Sneferu (also known as Snofru) was the first to attempt to build a true pyramid but the structure collapsed. The central core of this pyramid still stands at Maidum, south of Giza, but is surrounded by a huge pile of rubble.

Pharaoh Sneferu tried again, at a place called Dahshur, south of Giza. This pyramid is known as the Bent Pyramid because half way up, the angle of the walls changes. Snoferu finally built a true pyramid, the Red Pyramid, about a mile farther north.

Pharaoh Khufu (also known as Cheops) built the Great Pyramid at Giza.

The square base of the Castillo Pyramid, in the Mayan city of Chichén Itzá, was 55 m long and 30 m high. This is small compared with the Great Pyramid of Khufu at Giza, in Egypt, which is 230 m long and 146 m high.

The Step Pyramid at Saqqara in Egypt was constructed by Pharaoh Djoser's architect and Vizier, called Imhotep.

Pharaoh Menkaura (or Mycerinus) built the third and smallest of the Great Pyramids at Giza. It is called the Divine Pyramid.

Eight hundred spells for the dead were written in the burial chambers of some pyramids. These 'pyramid texts' were meant to protect the pharaoh from harm in the afterlife.

The river Nile used to flood the whole Nile valley each year, and this event was called the inundation. It occurred between June and September. Since the Aswan Dam was built in 1971, the river no longer floods.

Pharaoh Khafra (also known as Chephren) built the second pyramid at Giza. Khafra is also probably responsible for the Great Sphinx, since its face is noticeably similar to his.

The Nile is the longest river in the world, at 6,471 km.

31

Index